THESE ALEB WERE BROUGHT TO LIFE BY:

Alebrijes Coloring Book For Kids © 2019 by Nopalitos Publishing
All rights reserved. No part of this book may be used or reproduced in any manner whatsoever without written permission except in the case of brief quotations embodied in critical articles and reviews.
First edition: 2019

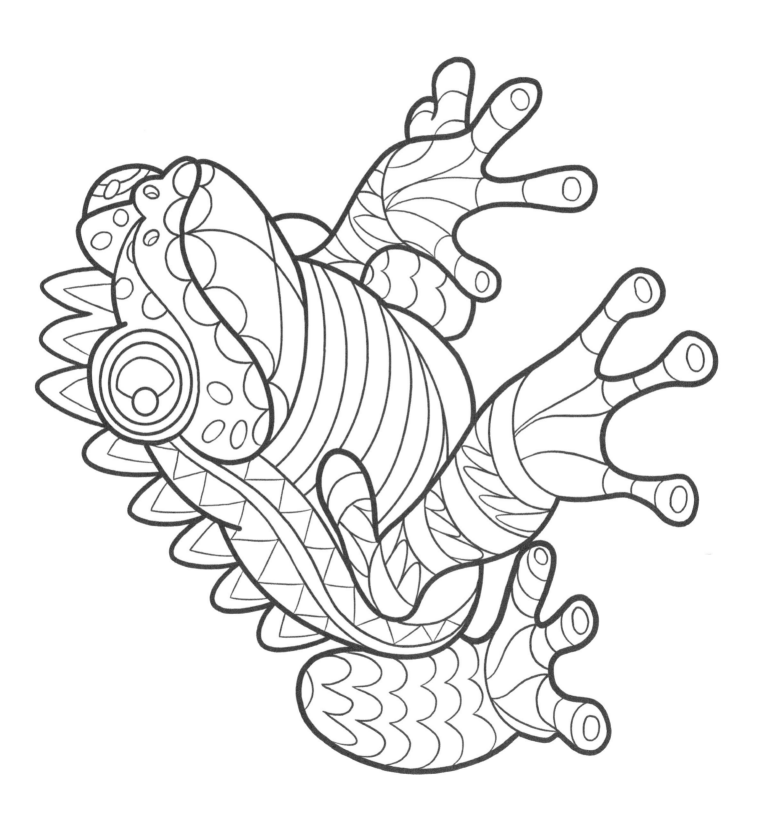

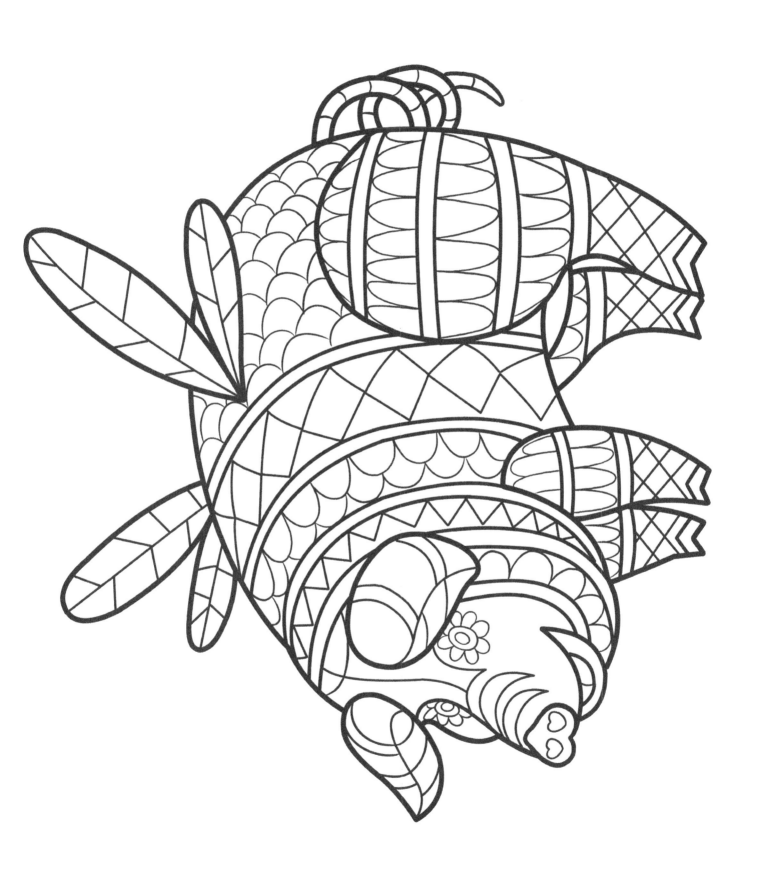

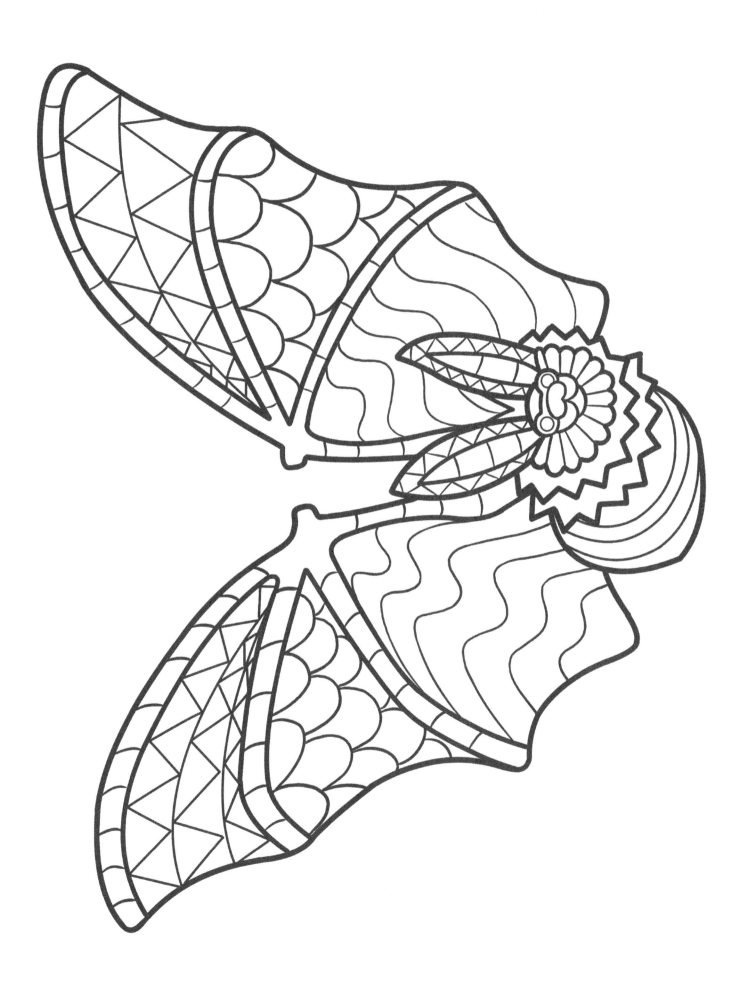

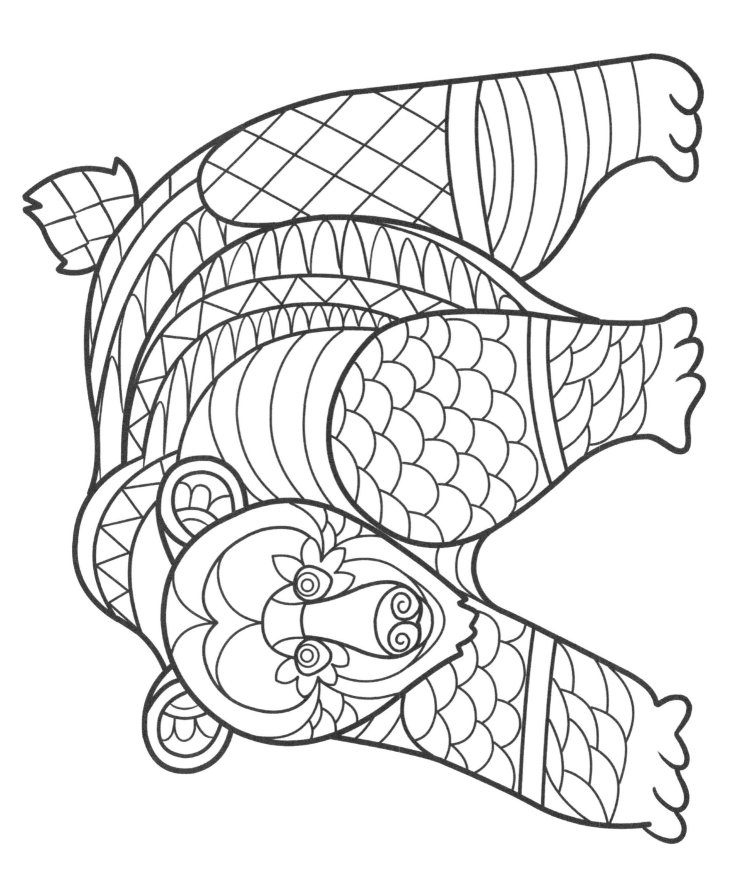

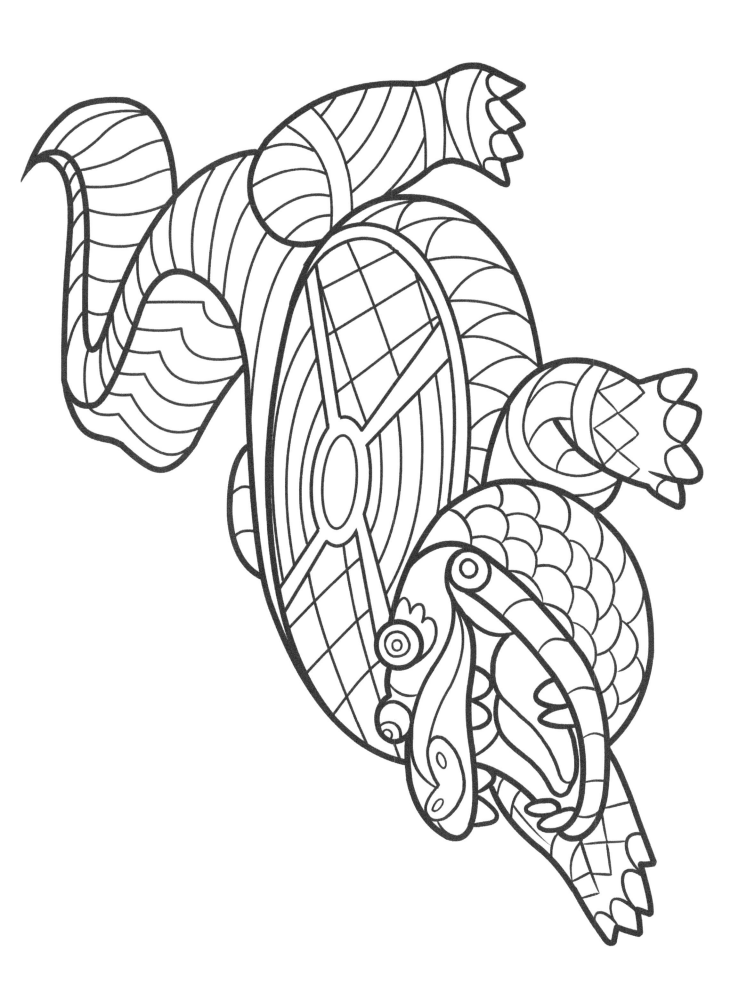

Made in the USA
Las Vegas, NV
02 September 2023

76953055R10037